4

Two wheels on a motorbike help people to get around.

Here at the quarry, Mr Slate gives us a lot of work to do. But the wheels and axles on these wheelbarrows make our work easier. The wheel turns around the axle. Together a wheel and axle help us do work while using less effort. Now that's the Fred Flintstone way!

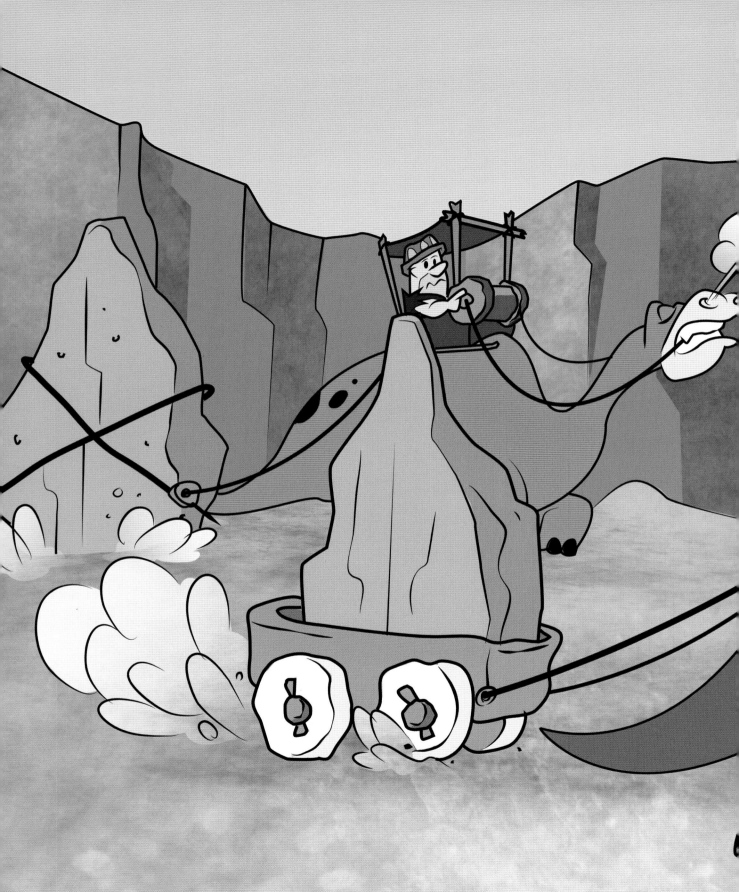

Wheels on a dumper truck make it easy to move tonnes of earth and rock.

Let me tell you about wheels and friction, Barney. Friction is a force that slows down motion. It happens when two things rub together or slide past each other.

Sure, Fred.

Just look at the poor pink dino! It's working hard to overcome friction. But the green one isn't working as hard. That's because wheels reduce friction.

Rocko's cart also helps make work easier to do. The cart and our wheelbarrows have wheels. The wheels cut down on friction when we move the rocks. When Rocko uses a cart, he doesn't have to work as hard.

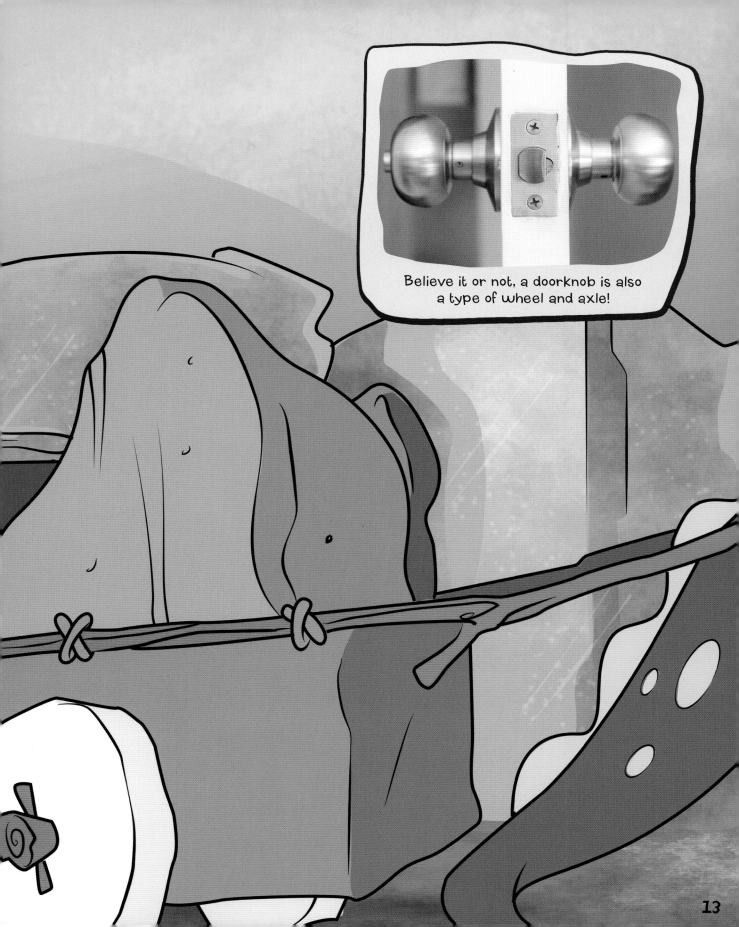

Big wheels enable tractors to do lots of heavy farm work.

In some parts of the world, big wheels are used to move boats along rivers.

Do you know where else we can see big steering wheels, Barney?

On buses and large sailing boats, Fred.

Wheels move us around. They can roll us down the driveway. They even give us a lift, especially when we step on them! But gravity always brings us back down. Wilma! Who left the skateboard lying around?

Wheels can be found on all types of fun things such as this skateboard.

Glossary

axle   bar in the centre of a wheel around which a wheel turns

effort   force applied to a machine to do work

force   push or pull exerted upon an object

friction   force produced when two objects rub against each other; friction slows down objects

gravity   force that pulls objects together

load   object that moves when a force is applied

quarry   place where stone or other minerals are dug from the ground

reduce   make something smaller or less in amount or size

valve   movable part that controls the flow of liquid or gas through a pipe

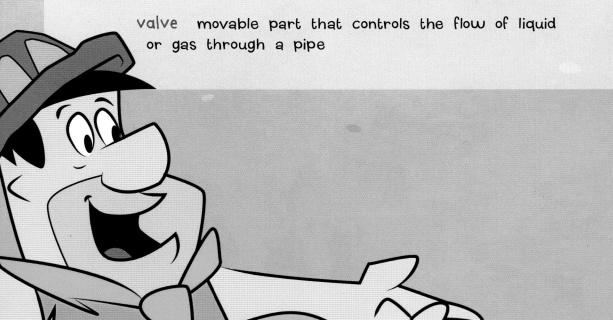

Read more

How Things Work (See Inside), Conrad Mason
(Usborne Publishing Ltd, 2009)

How Things Work Encyclopedia (First Reference), Dorling
Kindersley (DK Children, 2012)

Making Machines with Wheels and Axles (Simple Machine
Projects), Chris Oxlade (Raintree, 2015)

Website

www.dkfindout.com/uk/science/simple-machines/
Find out more about how we use simple machines.

Index

Look for all the books in the series:

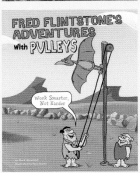

First published in 2016 by Curious Fox, an imprint of Capstone Global Library Limited, 264 Banbury Road, Oxford, OX2 7DY - Registered company number: 6695582

www.curious-fox.com

Copyright © 2016 Hanna-Barbera.
FLINTSTONES and all related characters and elements are trademarks of and © Hanna-Barbera.
WB SHIELD: ™ & © Warner Bros. Entertainment Inc. (s16) CAPS36557

Illustrations by Alan Brown

Printed and bound in China.
ISBN 978 1 78202 381 4
20 19 18 17 16
10 9 8 7 6 5 4 3 2 1

A CIP catalogue for this book is available from the British Library.

Edited by Alesha Halvorson
Designed by Ashlee Suker
Picture Research by Tracy Cummins
Production by Kathy McColley
Creative Director: Nathan Gassman

Acknowledgements
Shutterstock: dragunov, 9, oticki, 15, pudiq, 5, wittaya loysoungsin, 13; Thinkstock: Corepics VOF, 20, M_Arnold, 17

Thanks to our adviser for his expertise, research, and advice:
Paul Ohmann, PhD, Associate Professor of Physics
University of St. Thomas, St. Paul, Minnesota, USA

Every effort has been made to contact copyright holders of material reproduced in this book. Any omissions will be rectified in subsequent printings if notice is given to the publisher.

All the Internet addresses (URLs) given in this book were valid at the time of going to press. However, due to the dynamic nature of the Internet, some addresses may have changed, or sites may have changed or ceased to exist since publication. While the author and publisher regret any inconvenience this may cause readers, no reponsibility for any such changes can be accepted by either the author or the publisher.